source to resource

FROM
FIELD
TO
PLATE

MICHAEL BRIGHT

Crabtree Publishing Company
www.crabtreebooks.com

Crabtree Publishing Company
www.crabtreebooks.com
1-800-387-7650

Published in Canada
Crabtree Publishing
616 Welland Avenue
St. Catharines, ON
L2M 5V6

Published in the United States
Crabtree Publishing
PMB 59051
350 Fifth Ave, 59th Floor
New York, NY 10118

Author: Michael Bright

Editorial director: Kathy Middleton

Freelance editor: Katie Woolley

Editors: Annabel Stones, Liza Miller, and Ellen Rodger

Designer: Rocket Design Ltd

Proofreader: Wendy Scavuzzo

Prepress technician: Samara Parent

Print and production coordinator: Katherine Berti

Photographs:
p19 (bottom right): NASA

All other images and graphic elements courtesy of
Shutterstock

Illustrations:
Stefan Chabluk: p 14; p 30

Every effort has been made to clear copyright.
Should there be any inadvertent omission, please
apply to the publisher for rectification.

Published by Crabtree Publishing Company in 2017

The website addresses (URLs) included in this
book were valid at the time of going to press.
However, it is possible that contents or addresses
may have changed since the publication of this
book. No responsibility for any such changes can
be accepted by either the author or the publisher.

First published in 2016 by Wayland
(A division of Hachette Children's Books)
Copyright © Wayland, 2016

Printed in Canada/072016/PB20160525

Library and Archives Canada Cataloguing in Publication

Bright, Michael, author
　　　From field to plate / Michael Bright.

(Source to resource)
Includes index.
Issued in print and electronic formats.
ISBN 978-0-7787-2705-7 (hardback).--
ISBN 978-0-7787-2709-5 (paperback).--
ISBN 978-1-4271-1815-8 (html)

　　　1. Agricultural industries--Juvenile literature. 2 . Food industry
and trade--Juvenile literature. I. Title.

HD9000.5.B755 2016　　　j338.1'9　　　C2016-902588-8
　　　　　　　　　　　　　　　　　　　　　　　　　　　C2016-902589-6

Library of Congress Cataloging-in-Publication Data

Names: Bright, Michael, author.
Title: From field to plate / Michael Bright.
Description: New York, New York : Crabtree Publishing Company,
　　　2017. |
　Series: Source to resource | "First published in 2016 by Wayland" |
　　　Includes index.
Identifiers: LCCN 2016016661 (print) | LCCN 2016025533 (ebook) |
　　　ISBN 9780778727057 (reinforced library binding) |
　　　ISBN 9780778727095 (pbk.) |
　　　ISBN 9781427118158 (electronic HTML)
Subjects: LCSH: Food--Juvenile literature. | Food industry and
　　　trade--Juvenile literature. | Agriculture--Juvenile literature.
Classification: LCC TX355 .B75 2017 (print) | LCC TX355 (ebook) |
　　　DDC 641.3--dc23
LC record available at https://lccn.loc.gov/2016016661

Contents

Eat up!

At one time, the distance from field to plate was only a few miles. People bought foods in season from local markets, who were supplied by local farmers. Today, we can buy exotic foods from distant lands whenever we want. Food is traded across the world, so now the distance from field to plate can be thousands of miles!

A bit of everything

We eat food to provide our bodies with essential **nutrients** so we can grow and stay healthy. Humans are known as **omnivores**, or eaters of both meat and plants. Our early human **ancestors** got their food by hunting animals and collecting plants and **fungi** to eat.

Plants only

Some people choose not to be omnivores, and prefer to eat just plants, algae, and fungi, and nothing else. They are called vegans and vegetarians. Some vegetarians might also eat eggs and dairy products, such as cheese and yogurt, but neither vegans nor vegetarians eat meat.

A variety of good wholesome foods is essential for a healthy life.

Foods from around the world can now be easily enjoyed at home.

Tacos, meatballs, and noodles

The kinds of food we eat most are usually determined by where we come from. Chinese food is very different from Mexican food which, in turn, is different from Italian food. However, the food industry today has become so international that people can eat all these foods, at any time, in many cities around the world.

The right color

The color of food was important to our ancient ancestors. The color of fruit, for example, told them when it was ripe and ready to eat. Purple or green **mold** on food indicated it was rotting and unsafe to eat.

More recently, scientists wanted to see if color still affects the way we look at foods today. They colored foods such as freshly baked bread with purple, blue, and green edible dyes, and offered them to people. Nobody would eat them!

The blue-gray patches are a **fungus** called mold. It shows this bread is not safe to eat.

Food origins

Our earliest ancestors hunted wild animals and collected the tastiest plants, but it soon became clear that they could get more food, and more easily, if they looked after animals and controlled how plants grew. This was the start of agriculture, and the beginning of the journey from field to plate.

Tracing food origins

Many foods we eat every day have ancient origins. To find out when and where they first occurred, scientists study their **DNA**. DNA is in every living cell, and carries the instructions for what a plant or animal will be like and how it will grow. DNA also gives us an idea of what the ancestors of modern foods were like. DNA can tell us when and where people grew the first crops and raised the first animals, and it is surprisingly accurate.

Wild cattle

Ferocious wild cattle, known as the aurochs, were once scattered all over Europe and Asia. They were powerful and dangerous animals. These cattle were tamed by a brave farmer on an ancient farm in what is now Iran. All of today's cattle can be traced back to this single herd of just 80 animals that lived about 10,500 years ago.

Ancient peoples were afraid of wild bison and aurochs. The aurochs were eventually tamed, but the bison were not.

The ears of rice bend over with the weight of the ripening grains.

Wild rice

Rice was one of the earliest crops to be **cultivated**, and today it is a dietary **staple** for millions of people around the world. All varieties of rice can be traced back to one wild species that grew in the valley of the Pearl River in southern China, between 8,200 and 13,500 years ago.

Wild potatoes

Almost every variety of potato we grow today originally came from a type of wild potato that grew on the islands of the Chiloé Archipelago, off the coast of south-central Chile. It was brought to Europe by Spanish explorers in 1562, first to the Canary Islands, and later to mainland Europe.

Wild fowl

The red jungle fowl of India and Pakistan is the ancestor of all the chickens in Europe, the Americas, the Middle East, and Africa. The ancient Egyptians called it "the bird that gives birth every day." Asian chickens have a different jungle fowl ancestor.

In the field

Crop farmers are also known as arable land **farmers. They might grow grain, corn, or soybeans—in fact, just about any plant that we eat. The farmer's year is an exhausting, non-stop cycle of preparing the ground, planting, growing, and harvesting, and it is very dependent on the weather.**

Ancient crop

Barley was one of the earliest cereal crops grown by ancient peoples 10,000 years ago. It is easy to recognize because each grain of barley has a long spike, called an awn, growing out of it.

Barley grows well in cool conditions and, unlike wheat, even does well in nutrient-poor soil.

Grain harvesting

A combine harvester is used to harvest barley, wheat, and other cereal crops. It reaps or cuts the crop, threshes it to loosen the grain from the **husks** and leaves, and then winnows it to separate the grains from the rest of the plant. The stems and leaves, known as straw, are thrown out to be collected later, while the grain is poured into a truck to be transported away and used to make food, such as bread.

The barley grower's year

This is what a typical year might look like for a crop farmer growing spring barley in the United States and Canada.

LATE APRIL

Time to plow the ground. The plow turns and loosens the soil, buries the stalks from last year's crop, and prepares the soil for planting.

Drilling is the sowing of seeds in rows with a tractor and drill. The drill ensures that the seeds drop onto the ground at an even rate so they are not too close together or too far apart.

Flat metal rollers are then towed behind the tractor to firm up the seedbed, break up bits of soil, and reduce attacks by slugs.

JUNE

A battle rages in late spring and early summer as weeds and barley compete for living space and the goodness in the soil. Farmers help the barley by spraying a chemical called herbicide. It does not damage the barley, but it kills the weeds.

JULY/AUGUST

Damp weather can cause leaf rust and powdery mildew that will kill barley plants. These crop diseases are caused by fungi, so the farmer sprays a fungicide to protect the crops.

MAY

The crop starts to shoot up with the longer days of early spring. The first **fertilizer** is put on the field to help the crop grow.

AUGUST/SEPTEMBER

The sun is shining and it's harvest time. Barley grain is shipped for processing and then turned into bread, beer, and other foods. Straw is used for winter bedding for farm animals. Stalks are left in the field until plowing begins next year.

On the farm

Livestock farmers, also called pastoral farmers, raise cattle, hogs, chickens, and other animals. Like crop farmers, they raise their animals in a yearly cycle. Some also grow their own animal feed for the winter.

Dairy farming

Dairy farmers breed cows for milk, while beef farmers raise their cattle mainly for meat. Different breeds of cattle are raised to produce different farm products. For example, German black-and-white Holstein cows are kept for the large quantities of milk they produce, and the Japanese black wagyu is bred for high-quality beef.

Holstein dairy cows produce the most milk.

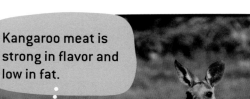

Kangaroo meat is strong in flavor and low in fat.

DID YOU KNOW?

While Australia is the natural home for kangaroos, people in other countries are increasingly raising them for meat to eat! The same is true for ostriches from Africa, water buffalo from Asia, alpacas and llamas from South America, and reindeer from Scandinavia.

The rancher's year

Here is a typical year in the life of a cattle rancher.

October/November

Ranchers grow crops such as oats, barley, and corn to feed their cattle. On northern ranches, the last of the crops are harvested in the fall. Silage, a type of cattle feed, is made from pasture grass.

March/April

On many ranches, calving season begins in February and lasts until mid-April. Ranchers and farmers work long hours. They even get up in the night to check on newborn calves.

December/January/February

Winter is spent repairing farm buildings such as calving sheds. These are shelters where cows deliver their calves.

Ranchers and farmers round up cattle to vaccinate them against disease.

May/June

Cattle are moved to open ranges, where they can roam and graze. Ranchers herd the cattle on horseback, with the help of cattle dogs.

July/August/September

While cattle are grazing on the range, ranchers and farmers round up strays and harvest winter feed crops that were planted in the spring.

11

Intensive farming

Regular farming gives nature a helping hand with fertilizers and pesticides, but industrial agriculture takes this even further. Large numbers of animals can be packed together to maximize the use of space, and large quantities of crops can be grown, even out of season.

Battery cage hens

Chickens are sometimes raised in row upon row of small cages. They have little room to move so they just sit, eat, and lay eggs. Many countries have banned this kind of **intensive farming**, but there are still some farmers that produce almost all of their eggs this way.

Pigpens

Some pigs are farmed indoors rather than being allowed to live and roam outside, as wild pigs would. Female pigs who are pregnant are put into sow stalls, which are barely wider than the pig, so it cannot turn around. When it is time to give birth, the mother pig is put in a farrowing stall. There she can lie down to suckle her piglets, but they are kept separate from her at other times. It prevents her from rolling over and crushing them, but she has little room to move. Many countries, such as the U.S., Canada, the European Union, and New Zealand have banned or are planning to ban this practice over the next few years.

Female chickens are kept in battery cages for their eggs. Males are killed immediately after hatching.

Greenhouses covering vast areas of the countryside.

The inside of a greenhouse is full of plants.

Fish farming

Some fish are raised in big tanks on land or in large, mesh enclosures in coastal waters. Tilapia, catfish, and carp are grown in tanks, ponds, and artificial lakes, while salmon and sea bass can be grown in enclosures in the sea. This type of farming has drawbacks, because having so many fish packed together allows **parasites** to spread easily, and large amounts of fish food creates pollution in the sea.

Greenhouses

In the past, in certain areas of North America, many vegetables and fruits were only available a few months of the year, due to the climate. Now, tomatoes, peppers, cucumbers, and other food crops can be grown in greenhouses. These structures absorb the sunlight and can also be heated, creating the perfect growing conditions to allow once-seasonal foods to be available all year long.

The sea louse is a salmon parasite.

13

Organic farming

Organic farming is very different from intensive farming. No chemical fertilizers or pesticides are used, and livestock must have access to pastures for grazing. In many countries, only farmers with a certificate from farm inspectors can claim their produce is organic.

Crop rotation

Organic farmers use **traditional** ways of farming that have changed very little through the centuries. Crop rotation is at the center of organic farming. This is when different crops are planted in a field each year to keep the soil **fertile**. One crop can benefit the next one. If the same crop was planted each year, pests would build up and nutrients in the soil would get used up. Crop rotation breaks the life cycles of pests and diseases.

A crop rotation sequence for one field could be wheat, then clover to increase nutrients, then corn, and then fallow for the field to recover.

Resting fields

Part of the crop rotation cycle is to leave some fields **fallow**, meaning they are plowed but not seeded. This allows the soil to recover. Alternatively, fields can be planted with special plants, such as clover, which add nutrients to the soil. In this way, the soil remains rich and fertile.

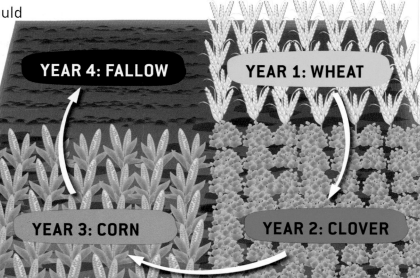

YEAR 4: FALLOW

YEAR 1: WHEAT

YEAR 3: CORN

YEAR 2: CLOVER

Free-range pigs love to sniff around and search for food!

Promoting growth and stopping pests

Organic farmers spread animal manure and **compost** on fields as natural fertilizers to boost plant growth. Local wildlife, such as insects, spiders, and birds, is encouraged to feed on pests as a form of natural pest control. It does not always work, so if pests do get out of control, certain pesticides made from natural sources may be used.

Happy animals

Livestock on organic farms is free range, which means during parts of the day the animals are free to roam the fields. Free-range cattle, sheep, pigs, and chickens appear to have less stress and less disease, which means they are healthier and need less medicine.

Organic pros and cons

PROS

- Natural habitats and wildlife are damaged less by organic farming.
- The soil tends to be in better condition.
- Experts say organic food is healthier, safer, and tastier.

CONS

- Insect pests and weeds are more likely to damage crops.
- Natural pesticides containing copper can be harmful to plants and worms.
- Crop **yield** is reduced.

Fresh foods

Transportation plays a vital role in getting food from the field to your plate. Some produce, such as grain, can be stored for a long time. However, most foods, such as fruit, vegetables, and fish, need to be transported quickly before they rot. Livestock needs to be taken to the abattoir with as little stress to the animals as possible.

Livestock to market

Shepherds use sheepdogs to herd their flocks down from the hills, and cattle are rounded up and put into pens. From here, they are loaded onto trucks or railway cars and taken to the abattoir to be killed.

Machine or hand-picked

Most crops are dug up or picked using mechanical harvesters. There are machines to shake fruit from trees, dig up potatoes and other root vegetables, and even separate the husks from rice grains. However, some crops, such as some grapes for wine, many tree fruits, and vanilla pods from orchids, are still harvested by hand.

In Europe, strict laws ensure farm animals are transported without injury and unnecessary suffering.

A constant temperature can be maintained inside a refrigerated shipping container.

Fishing

When fish is caught at sea, it is packed with ice to keep it fresh until the boats return home. At the dockside market, some fish is sold to local fishmongers and restaurants. The rest is loaded into refrigerated vans and trucks and sent to central fish markets, often located near ports. From there, fish and seafood are distributed to supermarkets, stores, and restaurants around North America.

International transport

Some crops, such as bananas, only grow in tropical places. Countries with warmer climates can grow crops all year long, so they supply produce out of season to countries with cooler climates. This means fruits and vegetables are transported around the world, usually in refrigerated ships, aircraft, and shipping containers. Cooling slows down the natural ripening process. The food is then fast-tracked through ports and airports.

Fresh fish have clear eyes and bright red gills.

Preserving food

Not all food is delivered fresh. For centuries, people have developed many ways to preserve food so that it can be stored. Some food can even be processed naturally to change it into something that is more nutritious or has a nicer taste.

Freezing

Freezing prevents chemicals called **enzymes** in food from working. The cold stops or slows the ripening and rotting process. Many foods are sold frozen, including fish, fruits, and vegetables.

Drying

Removing water slows the growth of **bacteria** in food and prevents rot. It is a method of preservation that can be traced back to at least 12,000 B.C.E. Fish, meat, fruits, and vegetables can all be dried.

Salting and pickling

Most bacteria die in salt, so rubbing salt on food or using salty water to pickle food is a popular method of preservation. Two of the oldest-known salted foods are fish such as salted cod, and salt-cured meat such as bacon.

Sugaring

Adding sugar to foods also kills bacteria. The process is used to turn fruits into jams, jellies, and marmalades, and to preserve vegetables such as ginger.

Canning

Food is also preserved by boiling, which kills bacteria. The food is then sealed in an airtight container. It can last a long time – in 1974, cans of food from a ship that sunk in the Missouri River in 1875 were tested. The food did not look good, but there was no bacterial growth, and it was considered safe to eat!

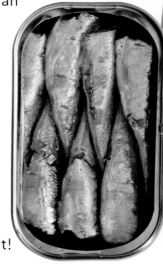

Smoking

Exposing food to wood smoke is a very old way of preserving it. The process dries the food, and chemicals in the smoke help to preserve it by killing bacteria. Wood smoking also adds a nice taste to foods such as smoked fish and smoked hams.

Space food

Astronauts rely on freeze-dried food. Freezing food rapidly and placing it in a vacuum preserves it. It can then be kept in a tube so it doesn't float away. Instant coffee and dried fruits in breakfast cereals are also preserved in this way.

Friendly bugs

Bacteria and fungi might seem to be enemies of the food industry, since they are part of the rotting process of food. Yet bacteria and a type of fungus called yeast are also used to preserve and process certain foods, such as bread and cheese.

Daily bread

Bread is probably the oldest human-made food. There is evidence that prehistoric people were making bread 30,000 years ago in southern Europe. To make simple flatbreads, they crushed grains, mixed them with water to form a paste, then cooked the mixture over fire.

The bread we eat today is also made from flour and water, but with the addition of yeast, which produces dough. When the dough is left to rest, the yeast causes the sugars and **starches** in the flour to **ferment**, which produces carbon dioxide. This makes the bread light and airy.

Bread rolls are made with the help of yeast.

Blue cheese has blue veins made by mold.

Nectar of the gods

To brew beer, wheat or barley is mixed with water and yeast, and to make wine, crushed grapes or other fruits are added to yeast. The starch in grain and the sugars in grapes are broken down and turned into alcohol by the yeast. Brewing is thought to have originated in ancient Mesopotamia (now Iraq) in 9,500 B.C.E., making beer the earliest alcoholic drink. The earliest record of wine is from 6,000 B.C.E. in Georgia, which is a country on the border between eastern Europe and Asia.

Say cheese

There is evidence that cheese was being made 7,500 years ago in Poland. Cheese is made from cow, goat, sheep, or buffalo milk, with the help of bacterias that either occur naturally in the milk or are added artificially. Rennet, an enzyme from the stomach of cattle, is added, which separates the milk into curds and whey. The whey is drained away and used to make foods such as whey butter, and the curd is used to make the cheese. Each type of cheese is prepared in a slightly different way. Blue cheese, for example, has a certain type of mold added to it, which gives the cheese its blue spots and veins.

Food for sale

Foods from farms, fishing boats, and bakeries eventually end up in stores, supermarkets, and restaurants. It is important that these foods reach their destination quickly, so that they are still fresh when sold or served.

Farm to supermarket

Supermarket chains buy some of their products directly from farmers at large distribution centers. The products are then packed onto trucks and delivered to individual stores. Some items are driven hundreds of miles before reaching your dinner plate.

Farmer's markets

Many farmers sell their products directly to the public at farmer's markets. These markets can be found in almost every village, town, or city. Vegetables, fruits, eggs, meat, fish, and poultry are just some of the items often found for sale by local farmers.

An indoor market in Asia.

Fruits and vegetables at a supermarket are often carefully selected to look the same in shape, size, and color.

Fruits and vegetables at a farmer's market are often found in different shapes, colors, and sizes — sometimes even strange ones!

Specialty food shops

While supermarkets tend to stock just about everything you need at home, some smaller stores specialize in selling only certain foods. Here are a few:

- **Butchers** sell meat, poultry, and eggs.

- **Fishmongers** sell fish and shellfish.

- **Cheese shops** sell specialty cheeses.

- **Bakeries** make and sell flour-based foods, such as breads, cakes, pastries, and pies.

- **Delicatessens** sell cold cuts, cheeses, and many prepared foods, such as salads, sandwiches, or cooked meats. Some specialize in foods from a particular country or culture, such as Italian or Jewish food.

The best cuts

Many foods arrive at stores in packaging, but inside the package, most foods have changed little in appearance from when they left the farm. Meat is different. A carcass of beef, lamb, or pork must be sliced into smaller pieces. Butchers in different countries cut up meat in different ways, and they give each piece its own special name. In North America, for example, the rib-eye steak is a cut of beef from the rib section of the cow. This steak is also known as a Scotch fillet in Australia, or an entrecôte in France.

Preparing food

The last stage of the journey from field to plate is in the kitchen. Some foods are eaten raw, while others are cooked using heat. Cooking food helps to break it down, making it easier to digest, and sometimes releases more nutrients.

 There are several basic techniques used in modern cooking.

Boiling is the process of cooking food in boiling water or any other hot, water-based liquid, such as milk or stock. A gentle boil is called simmering. If the liquid moves without forming bubbles, it is called poaching.

Frying is cooking food in oil or fat. It can be animal fat, such as lard or butter, or plant oil, such as coconut oil or grapeseed oil. It is a type of cooking that started in ancient Egypt, in about 2,500 B.C.E.

Grilling uses dry heat, sometimes from an open fire, that cooks food on one side at a time. The food can be on an open wire grill or in a grill pan with raised ridges.

BOILING

FRYING

GRILLING

Baking uses dry heat in an oven to cook breads, cakes, and pastries. Heat travels from the surface of the food to the inside, so the outside is often a dry crust, while the center is soft.

Roasting uses dry heat, usually in an oven. Very hot air, at a temperature of at least 300 °F (150 °C), surrounds the food and cooks it evenly.

Steaming relies on water boiling continuously to form steam. The steam surrounds the food and cooks it. Some people think it is the healthiest way to cook food, because it allows vegetables and meats to keep their nutrients. Some nutrients are lost in other forms of cooking.

A zillion-dollar lobster frittata

Food can be fun, but also pricey. The world's most expensive omelette is found at Norma's Restaurant in New York. It is lobster on a bed of fried potatoes covered with egg and topped with expensive Sevruga caviar. The supersize frittata costs about $1,000!

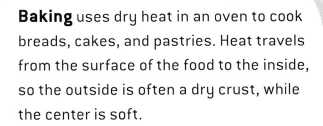

BAKING

STEAMING

ROASTING

Safe food

Food is the perfect place for bacteria to grow. The bacteria in food can cause food poisoning, or the food can carry other diseases, such as typhoid, from one person to another. The World Health Organization has noted five key ways to help keep food safe.

1. Keep clean

- Dangerous **microbes** are carried on hands, dish cloths, cooking pots and pans, and cutting boards. They can easily be transferred to food.

- Wash your hands before handling food.

- Wash cooking equipment and surfaces.

- Protect kitchen areas from insect pests and other animals.

2. Separate raw and cooked

- Raw animal products, such as meat, poultry, and seafood, as well as their juices, can carry microbes that **contaminate** other foods.

- Separate raw meat, poultry, and seafood from other foods.

- Use separate knives and cutting boards for preparing raw foods.

- Store food in containers to avoid contact between raw and prepared foods.

3. Cook thoroughly

- Proper cooking, to a temperature of at least 158 °F (70 °C), kills most dangerous microbes.

- Cook food thoroughly, especially meat, poultry, eggs, and seafood.

- Always bring soups and stews to a boil.

- After cooking, make sure the juices of meat and poultry run clear, not pink.

Chicken is fully cooked when its juices run clear. •••••••••

A kitchen must be cleaned after the preparation of every meal or bacteria can be spread.

4. Store food at safe temperatures

- Microbes **reproduce** rapidly in foods stored at room temperature, and some will still grow in the fridge.

- Do not leave cooked food at room temperature for more than two hours.

- Put cooked and **perishable** food in the fridge quickly, but do not store it there for too long.

- Keep cooked food piping hot, at more than 140 °F (60 °C), before serving.

5. Use safe water and foods

- Some uncooked foods can be contaminated with microbes, and damaged or moldy raw foods can contain dangerous chemicals.

- Use clean drinking water and select fresh foods.

- Choose foods that have been made safe, such as **pasteurized** milk.

- Wash fruit and vegetables, especially if eaten raw.

World food

Global food consumption is generally on the rise, with more people in developing countries having access to adequate food supplies. Even so, at least 165 million children around the world do not have enough food to eat.

The wrong foods

Having more food does not necessarily mean a healthier life. In many countries, diets have changed to include more processed foods, such as fast food, with high levels of fat and sugar. This has led to **obesity** and a higher incidence of dangerous diseases, such as heart disease and diabetes.

Food waste

It may come as a surprise to learn that in developed countries, such as the United States, more than 30 percent of food is wasted. The amount of food wasted is about four times the amount of food imported, or brought in, by poorer developing nations in Africa.

Fast foods tend to have high levels of salt that can cause dangerously high blood pressure in some people.

Many households in North America are very wasteful. On average, one in three bags of food goes straight in the trash and off to the dump.

Saving seeds

As an insurance policy against diseases wiping out the world's crops, seeds from all the plants on Earth are stored in special seed banks. The largest in the world are the Millenium Seed Bank, near London, U.K., and the Svalbard Global Seed Vault in Norway. They both house billions of seeds in underground vaults that would survive a nuclear war or similar disaster.

Loss of food varieties

Three-quarters of the world's food is obtained from only 12 plants—such as rice, corn, and wheat—and five animal species: cows, sheep, pigs, goats, and chickens. Many farmers have replaced their local varieties of crops with fewer high-yield varieties. Ancient breeds of farm animals have been lost in favor of the few that provide more meat. If diseases hit these modern crops and farm animals, the world would have little left to eat. Fortunately, some farmers are trying to preserve the old breeds and grow the old crops, so the future for food looks bright.

This is the Svalbard Global Seed Vault in Arctic Norway.

Further information

BOOKS

Foods in Different Places by Linda Barghoorn, Crabtree Publishing, 2016

From Farm to Table: Food and Farming by Richard and Louise Spilsbury, Wayland, 2010

Life in a Farming Community by Lizann Flatt, Crabtree Publishing, 2010

Sustainable Farming: How Can We Save Our World? by Carol Ballard, Franklin Watts, 2009

WEBSITES

Visit this website for fun facts about where food comes from:
www.myamericanfarm.org

Check out this website for videos, lessons, and games about food and farming:
www.neok12.com/Agriculture.htm

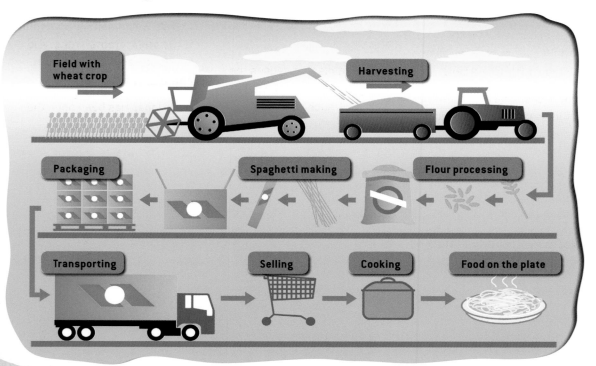

Glossary

abattoir A place where animals are slaughtered

ancestor A person who lived before you, to whom you are related

arable land Land that is good for growing crops

bacteria Microscopic living things, some of which can cause disease

compost A mixture of dead plant material that has rotted and broken down, and is used to improve the quality of soil

contaminate To make unclean

cultivate To improve growth

DNA Deoxyribonucleic acid, a complex molecule that is the blueprint for life, containing all the instructions for building cells

enzyme A chemical produced by living things that helps chemical reactions, such as the digestion of food, to take place

fallow Describes a piece of land that has been plowed and left to rest

ferment Convert sugar to carbon dioxide and alcohol through a chemical reaction caused by

microscopic living things, such as yeasts

fertile Able to produce crops in large quantities

fertilizer A chemical that makes the soil more productive

fungus Part of a group of plant-like living things that includes mushrooms, mold, and yeast

husk The outer covering of seeds, such as rice grains

intensive farming The production of crops with artificial fertilizers and pesticides. Also, cramming animals together to produce as much as possible.

microbe A microscopic living thing, for example, bacteria that can cause disease

mold A fungus that causes the furry growth on rotting food. Some food, such as blue cheese, have mold added to it for taste.

nutrient A substance in food that is needed by your body to stay healthy and to grow

omnivore A person or animal that eats food from both plants and animals

obesity An excess of bodyweight caused by eating too much food or unhealthy foods

parasite A species that lives in a relationship with another species in which the host is harmed

pasteurize To expose a substance to high temperatures to reduce the number of dangerous microbes

perishable Describes something that rots quickly

reproduce To make something that is the same or very similar to something else

staple A main or important item, especially in one's diet

starch A common nutrient found in the stems, roots, fruits, and seeds of plants, such as corn, potatoes, wheat, and rice

traditional Has been done the same way for many years

yield The total amount of a crop or product produced

Index